Master How Strong And Ducks

Complete Guide On How To Raise Ducks In Your Backyard

Yolanda Barrett

Introduction

Ducks are some of the most adorable creatures. Picture this; it's Saturday, and you're walking in the park enjoying your day, watching all the people having fun with their dogs and families. You make your way to one of the benches near the pond but before you get there, you hear a commotion behind you. When you look back, you see some teenagers filming the cutest and most endearing scene you've ever seen.

A mother duck, and some of her ducklings are stuck at the rift between the path and the curb. What makes the scene so endearing is that as you watch, the mother duck jumps over the curb and lands on the path. This prompts some wild cheers from the crowd, which starts to get bigger. As you watch, the mother duck quacks, and the baby ducklings follow their mother's cues and start jumping over the curb and into the pathway that le1ads straight to the pond. As each duckling jumps over, stumbles, staggers, and gets to its feet, you can't help but wonder, "How cute is that?"

Have you ever harbored thoughts of raising ducks but were too afraid to get started? If you can relate to the above scene and question, I have some thrilling news for you: raising ducks, no, raising strong healthy ducks as pets or for profits is easier than you may have thought or led to believe. In fact, getting started and being on your way to being a proud duck owner is as easy as raising chicken if not easier.

Here is the thing: at this particular moment, you may be asking yourself this question: "should I get into duck farming/raising?" "What exactly goes into raising strong healthy ducks?"

The truth is that a lot goes into raising strong healthy ducks. Don't let this intimidate or scare you, even if you've never stepped foot on a farm or know a thing about keeping ducks. If you've ever had a pet, be it a fish, dog, or whatever, you can raise strong and healthy ducks as pets or for other reasons (for meat or egg purposes, or for commercial reasons).

This brings us to today. How can you raise strong, healthy ducks? That is precisely what this book intends to teach you. This book will teach you everything there is to know about duck raising. It will do so in the following modules.

Introduction To Duck Raising

In this chapter, we shall look at and delve into everything about duck raising. We shall look at duck breeds so that you can have a firm understanding of the type of duck best suited to you, depending on your goal. We shall also look at basic duck care, touch on how many ducks you should start with and cap all this off with duck care on the way home.

Duck Housing 101

In this chapter, we shall learn everything there is to learn about duck housing. We shall also look at some basic duck care where we'll cover the basics of duck care in relation to the best environment and conditions best for raising strong healthy ducks.

After covering this, we shall move to:

The Ins And Outs Of Duck Feeding

In this chapter, we shall delve into everything feeding. We shall look at what and how to feed your ducklings at various stages of their development. When we're done with this, we shall then move to;

How To Raise Strong Healthy Ducks

In this chapter, we shall look at how to keep your ducks healthy and diseases free. This combined with the knowledge of how to feed your ducks will tie in together towards the success of your duck raising goals.

In the last chapter "How to implement what you've learnt", we shall recap everything we have learnt in five or less easy steps you can jump to anytime and implement at any moment of your duck rearing journey.

If you're as excited as I am, let's get started.

Table of Contents

Duck Raising 101: Introduction To Duck Raising

"If you know anything about ducks, you know a baby duck will imprint itself on you. It misses its mother"

- Michael Leunig

Have you ever raised chicken before? If you have, you're at a bit of an advantage because raising ducks is almost similar to raising chicks.

Contrary to the myth, ducks don't necessarily need a huge pond for them to grow healthy and flourish. In fact, the only thing ducks require is a clean environment with some form of swimming mechanism to keep them happy (the swimming mechanism in this case could be a large bowl, kiddie pool, river, pond, or even trough).

Ducks are very friendly, intelligent and compassionate pets. If we do a side-by-side comparison to other domestic fouls, ducks are more useful and versatile than most because they serve multiple purposes. For example, ducks lay eggs, provide meat, nutritious fertilizers, and act as a form of pest control.

Generally, ducks are a very popular animal. To know what I mean, just go to YouTube.com and search for duck videos. The results will be adorable and sometimes funny duck videos with some of the videos having over three million hits.

One of the most amazing things about ducks is that on top of giving you a steady supply of eggs rich in omega-3, they are great animal companions. If you're reading this, it probably means that you're keen on raising ducks. As we have seen, ducks are very versatile and useful animals to have around. Although there are many reasons why you'd want to raise ducks, allow me to outline some reasons why your decision to start raising ducks is a wise choice.

Advantages Of Duck Raising

As we have indicated, there are many reasons that would motivate one to rear ducks. Here is the truth though; before your ducks can start paying you back in the various ways we shall look at shortly, you have to take care of them. I'm not going to lie to you that it's easy. If you've had any experience with rearing chicks, you know this. However, what I'm going to tell you, and hopefully show you later is that when you know what you're doing, duck raising is one of the easiest things you can do. Further, ducks, ducklings or otherwise add a ton of advantages to our lives.

Some of these advantages are:

Ducks Produce Tastier Eggs

Do you like chicken eggs? If yes, then you will really love duck eggs. They're richer and contain more calcium, potassium, protein, iron, vitamin A, and folate and pretty much of major minerals compared to many other eggs. A duck egg contains a big yolk, which means more proteins.

In addition, because a duck egg is double the size of a chicken egg, it has more egg whites. Duck eggs are some of the best eggs to use for baking because when you bake with them, the significant amount of egg whites makes the baked foods like cakes rise airy and high; the cakes also tend to have a more fluffy texture. Cookies baked with duck eggs are moister and tend to be chewier. The egg whites (albumen) of ducks are much more firm than those of chicken: hence, this property helps in binding of ingredients together in your food and improves the texture of the baked foods.

Duck eggs also have more fat content - the good kind of fat. This is actually a very good thing because the fats in duck eggs are monounsaturated and polyunsaturated fats. Unsaturated fats are healthy fats that your body requires to keep you healthy and well. It also contains a higher concentration of Omega 3 fatty acids (about 72 mg per egg).

Omega 3 is very important nutrient because it:

- Lowers blood pressure

- Reduces triglycerides in your body

- Reduces the likelihood of heart attacks and stroke

- Reduces or treats depression and anxiety

- Improves eye and brain health,

- Helps in preventing cancer cases

- And much more

Raising ducks will help you save up a chunk of the money you might use to get Omega 3 supplements.

One of the many advantages to this lies in the fact that ducks can lay more eggs per year (approximately 200 to about 250 eggs) always, until they reach old age (that is around 7 or 8 years). Changes in seasons (like winter), do not affect their egg production tendencies; therefore, this makes them better egg producers than any other domesticated foul.

One more beautiful thing about ducks is that they will never eat their own eggs the way chickens sometimes do.

Ducks Are Low Maintenance

Ducks thrive on the same foods like many other domesticated fouls like corn, wheat, oats, rice, etc. Amazingly, remember when we talked about ducks being versatile; part of the reason for this is that ducks will graze and forage for a higher percentage of their own food. This translates into less work for you and reduced expenses when raising them. Ducks will get most of their feeds by themselves through foraging; you will probably just feed commercial feeders in the evening when they get back to their pen for the night.

Moreover, ducks take less space. They do not fly, and they love to be closer together. In fact, three to four square feet per hen is enough for their house. Their tendency to forage a lot the whole day makes it easier to keep their habitat clean; therefore, you don't need to change their straw bedding as often as you would do for chicken.

Ducks Are Hardier

Ducks are literally the toughest kind of poultry. They have a stronger immune system and are always healthy. They can spend their entire life not falling sick or affected in any way.

They have an internal temperature of 41.7° C (107°F), which makes their bodies inhospitable to most bacteria, viruses or any other internal parasites. They also don't need vaccinations or annual shots of medicinal drugs.

They do not fall sick easily and are not susceptible to most chicken diseases like coccidiosis, Marek's diseases, etc. Ducks can get Avian flu but are not affected it. They can only be carriers of the avian flu when they contract it.

What's more; their tendency to spend most of their time in water makes them less susceptible to external parasites such as lice, mites, ticks, fleas, etc.

Ducks Are Good For Your Garden

Did you know ducks are relentless pest hunters? They are. Ducks love pests. They especially love slugs and snails. Slug and snails are tomato plant or any alluring plant killers.

If you release ducks on your shaded garden, they will leave the place free of slugs. If you have a tomato patch and release your ducks there, there will be no hornworm in sight. Fortunately, ducks are bit more intelligent than chicken. In fact, ducks will not disturb your garden plants by scratching the ground.

In addition to bugs, ducks will also eat weeds and grass in your garden. After harvesting, let your ducks forage around your garden and they will do the job of cleaning up your garden before the next planting season.

Furthermore, the water from the ducks' pool is very nutritious for your plants. You can use it to water your plants and provide a cleaner one for them. This is literally the perfect example of a good symbiotic relationship.

Ducks Provide Good Fertilizer For Your Garden Soil

While they are cleaning up your garden from bugs and weeds, ducks will also provide manure for the soil in your garden as they graze around.

Duck poop a lot and continuously. They do not have the lower sphincter muscles in their gut; therefore, they can't control their bowel movements. Their poop is liquid in nature, which makes it easier to disperse into the soil.

Duck droppings have a high nutrient content. They have the most nutritious poop when compared to other domestic livestock. The nitrogen, phosphate, and potassium ratio is higher, almost like the NPK fertilizer you would buy from a store. This essentially means rearing ducks is very beneficial when you also have a farm around your home.

Ducks Are Quieter And Have A Phlegmatic Temperament

Drakes (male ducks), unlike chicken roosters, do not make any loud sounds at all. They basically just make something like a soft, raspy, or a hissing sound that is much calmer and nice to hear. They do not crow in the morning the way roosters do. Drakes are very calm and peaceful.

Female ducks, on the other hand, are louder than the drakes; their quacks are much louder but not as compared to those of chicken. When they lay eggs, they do not shout it out to the world the way chickens do.

Ducks are the most recommended to raise in a closer neighborhood because they won't disturb the peace of your neighbors. They are heavy, and they can't fly; hence, they will stay only in your yard as long as you have a fence around your home.

Ducks are social animals; they are calm, intelligent, and peaceful birds. They get lonely and depressed when caged or left alone; that is why it is advisable to keep a flock. They get along well with people and are safe around kids since they don't peck people. Make them get used to you as their owner, to make their handling easy.

Ducks easily accept a new flock when introduced. They are friendly and welcoming to their fellow ducks. In simple terms, for ducks, "the more the merrier". They are also much easier to herd.

Ducks Do Not Require Unique Housing Facilities

Ducks do not need roosting perches or nesting boxes or continuous unique lighting system; just a simple shade that can protect against predators is enough for them. The cost and simplicity of building a duck shelter is way lower as compared to building a chicken coop or any other pet animal or livestock. Just ensure that you have a well-ventilated area and good bedding for your ducks, and they will be comfortable enough to stay.

Most people will turn their dog house into a duck house. And the ducks will be comfortable in that area. Ducks do not demand much; that's why they are more advantageous over other poultry.

Ducks Are Good For Business.

Ducks grow fast as compared to chicken, they are heavier and their meat is leaner and more delicious. Ducks' eggs are larger and more nutritious. One drake can manage to fertilize around 6 female ducks with ease. And more importantly, they are much cheaper to raise.

Duck eggs and meat are sold at a higher price compared to chicken. They live longer and are not affected by different conditions. They will ensure your customers get their weekly supply of eggs throughout the year.

Ducks Are Fun To Watch

Earlier on, I asked you to head over to YouTube.com and do a "duck video" keyword search. If you did, I have a question for you. Did you enjoy those adorable, funny, and sometimes dangerous duck videos?

Many of us love bird watching. We think its a fun thing. When it comes to ducks, watching them is immensely entertaining. They love swimming and will have fun in anything from a kiddie pool to a dishpan. In fact, contrary to popular belief, the only thing ducks need to be happy is a deep enough pool that allows them to dip their entire head. Ducks love dipping their head in the water and do it with a lot of enthusiasm and frequency.

If you will get yourself an ornamental duck like the wood duck, Eurasian duck, mandarin duck, or the mallard duck:

you will find yourself addicted to their beauty and the way they conduct themselves.

Furthermore, it is amusing to watch how ducks mingle with each other, male and female duck courtship, or how mother ducks care for and guide their ducklings.

If you had no interest in duck raising, I'm hopeful that this bit of our learning process has rekindled your passion for duck raising, and you're now ready to get started.

Before you can raise ducks for whatever reason, you should know the type of ducks available. I find that this is especially useful in helping you decide which type of duck best suits your needs and duck raising goals.

Let us take a brief look at the types of ducks available to you.

Types Of Duck: The Best Duck Breeds For Beginners

When it comes to raising ducks, there are many types of breeds. As a novice' duck-owner to be,' chances are high that you feel overwhelmed when it comes to choosing which duck breed best suits you and which one you should go for.

Your choice to raise ducks will come from the question of, "why do you want to keep ducks?" Having that question in your mind, you will be able to distinguish the duck breed that will suit you.

Sit down and ask yourself these questions; "do I want to rear ducks for egg production, or do I want them for meat production?" Do I want to do it on a short scale or do I want to do it for commercial purposes.

The answer to these questions will vary from person-to-person depending on various things such as:

- How much space one has

- If they're doing duck raising as a pet project. Some ducks are friendly and easily interact with people. For instance, some breeds like the Swedish breed are best for being

19

pets because of their calm demeanor; while others do not connect with people at all.

- Some duck breeds are best for egg production; whereas others are very good at meat production. However, most breeds serve both purposes.

- Some people raise ducks for commercial reasons

- And most importantly, how much resource is at one's disposal. Because your resources will determine the number of ducks you will raise.

The Following Are The Common Types Of Duck Breeds

Muscovy Duck Breed

Muscovy ducks are a good multipurpose duck breed. Their meat is the best flavor and tastes wonderful. The Muscovy duck breed belongs to 'Genus-Carina', which has its roots of origin in South America.

It comes in several colors, but most of them are white in color. Other common colors include the pied (which is a mixture of white and black color), brown, buff color, chocolate, blue and finally lilac.

It is a multipurpose duck breed because it is a medium egg producer and when it is young, it is hardy and easy to rear.

It is ideal for someone with a backyard because it's a good grazer and forager. Amazingly, the male Muscovy can grow large to the extent of weighing 4.5-5.5 kilograms, while a smaller female can weigh anywhere from 2.3-2.8 kilograms. These duck breeds grows fast and becomes marketable at the age of 12 weeks.

They live for 8 to 12 years.

Characteristics Of The Muscovy Duck Breed.

Muscovy duck has several distinguishing characteristics from other duck breeds. For example:

If it has already mated with a member of its breed, it will not mate with a member from another breed. It is broody in such a way that it will sit on its own eggs and eggs from other ducks until they hatch.

Muscovy ducks are good at flying. Most of the time, you will find them perching on trees (they have well developed talons for this purpose). So when you are building a shelter for them, make sure you include roosts, which they will use to sleep on at night.

If you are living in an urban area, I would recommend you to clip off the third section of your Muscovy ducks when they are a week old; otherwise, they will fly off, interfere with your neighbors' peace or even get lost. They don't swim much, unlike other ducks.

They are quiet birds. Male Muscovy's will hiss instead of quacking; while the female will make something like a soft cooing sound. This makes them a perfect breed for the close neighborhood.

When cross mating is successful, the crossbred offspring, referred to as mules, are infertile. Some people use these mules purely for meat purposes.

Muscovy meat is considered the best meat on the market. Their meat is very lean, with at least 98 percent fat-free. You will get a protein-rich meal when you eat this meat. Their meat has a rich taste, nutritious, and is very delicious.

The Muscovy is poor in egg production and lays most of its eggs in clutches. It can lay 20 or more eggs and stay awhile before producing eggs again. Its eggs go for 35 days before hatching, while those of other duck breeds take about 28 days. Its meat has lower fat content compared to other duck breeds.

Being foragers, Muscovy ducks will search for and eat weeds, algae from water bodies like ponds, slugs, bugs, ants, flies, maggots, mosquitoes, mosquito larva, spiders and practically anything that crawls and creeps. They are the best breed for pest control purposes.

Pekin

This white duck was developed in China in 1872, after which it was distributed globally. The American Pekin duck breed is the perfect breed for commercial purposes. This is because it is good for egg production and hatchability.

It is the most popular breed in North America. The Pekin duck grows fast and is rather beautiful to look at because of its white creamy feather. It adapts well to confinement and has natural hardiness and diseases resistance compared to other duck breeds.

It has a calm temperament and interacts well with people. It also has good meat yield and distinct flavor as well. The Pekin is marketable at 7 weeks, weighing about 3.5kgs.

Pekin ducks will give you about 150 large, delicious eggs per year for 8 to 12 years.

In addition, mule (the result of crossbreeding female Pekin and male Muscovy), has good lean meat yields, with a luscious flavor. The crossbreed grows faster than the Muscovy. Unfortunately, the crossbreed is sterile and only becomes marketable at 8 weeks of age.

Rouen Duck

Rouen duck is a really old breed of duck that originated from France. This duck is not a good choice for commercial purposes because they take almost a year to reach their full size. But as a farmer, it is practical to keep some for meat purposes.

Although they are heavy and provides a good source of meat and eggs, they are kept mainly for exhibition due to their beautiful plumage. They come in white color, blue or apricot (light yellowish orange-ish color).

Rouen ducks have a large body with a flat-like base (due to their horizontal carriage) and a back aching from its shoulder to the tail. This gives it a block-like body. The drake has black eyes, dark yellow bill, and light orange shanks and feet while the Rouen duck has a brown bill, dark orange shanks and feet.

Rouen duck can be confused with the mallard breed because they almost look alike. Rouen are significantly larger in size as compared to the mallards. They also differ in the number of black stripes on their face; Rouen has 2 black stripes, one across the eye and the other one is under the eye. Mallards have only one black stripe on their face. Make sure you get the exact bird that you need because if you are not keen, you can pick a mallard instead of the Rouen.

Rouen ducks are poor layers; they will give you 60 to 140 eggs per year. And may reach up to 9 to 10 pounds in weight, making it a good source of a delicious meat.

Rouen duck is calm, sociable and they make good entertaining pets. They are great waterfowls; therefore, make sure you have a water body around like a kiddie pool, trough, etc. because they really love to swim.

Indian Runner

These ducks are known mostly by the way they stand. They stand erect like penguins. This is due to their upright carriage. Their pelvic girdle is situated more towards their tail region.

They have a unique upward stance (with an angle of 50 to 70 degrees upwards).

Indian runners are lightweight ducks, weighing around 4 to 5 lbs.; they are slender and have a long neck and an upright back. The legs are set far back towards the tail. They are the tallest duck species, approximately 20 to 30 inches in height.

The ducks have flat tails while the drakes have a curl at the top of their tails.

They come in a variety of colors, but the common ones are apricot, buff, black, blue, white, grey, etc.

Indian runner ducks are the best egg layers. They are bred mostly for egg laying purposes. Their eggs are very nutritious since they are one of the best foragers. They eat a variety of insects, worms, seeds, slug and bugs, snails etc. This explains why they are also kept for pest control.

Indian runners will give you 300 to 350 greenish-white eggs per year. They start laying when they are 4 ½ months old and lay consistently through the different seasons. They don't usually sit on their eggs, so if you want some to hatch, use artificial incubators or place them under other brooding ducks like the Cayuga breed. They will live for more than 10 years if you take good care of them.

They like to swim but sometimes they do spend almost their entire day foraging for food and might go without swimming. But it is advisable to have a container or a small pond for them to swim in when they feel like it.

This breed was first spotted in the Indonesian island in Asia, as early as the 1600s.

Khaki Campbell

The khaki Campbell is a British breed, developed in England in 1901. They were made by crossing the Indian runner, Rouen and the mallard breeds.

They come mostly in khaki color, as their name suggests, but other very few Campbell strains are white and sometimes black.

Khaki Campbell are very easy and economical to raise. They are the best choice for commercial purposes. And being a cross, they are good at both egg-laying and meat production.

Khaki Campbells mature at about 7 months. Their egg production capability exceeds even the best egg-laying chickens in the world. They are easy to manage because they lay their eggs in the morning hours around 9 O'clock. And they will give you as many as 340 eggs per year.

And in addition to that, they will provide you with delicious meat for you and your family or friends. The drakes weigh 4 to 5 pounds while the ducks weigh about 3.5 pounds. And to sweeten things up more for you, khaki Campbell will live for 10 to 15 years.

Khaki Campbell breed are very friendly, strong, and energetic, and they also have a good temperament. They adapt easily and can thrive in any climate or weather.

They are good foragers, and are hardy birds. They do not fall sick easily: that's why they are very economical to raise and are very profitable birds for commercial purposes. Their cost of production is very low but they will give you huge profits when you sell them, their eggs or their meat.

Adult ducks love and enjoy swimming and breeding; therefore, water is a must for mating and breeding. Build a small pond for them or use a bathtub if you have one. Even plastic kiddie pools are a good choice. Just make sure there is always water around because these ducks can't live without sufficient water.

Crested Ducks

If you have ever seen a duck with a tuft of feathers on top of their heads, then you know this breed. This tuft of feathers is brought about by genetic mutation that brings about a deformity in their skull. They originated from the East Indies and were brought to Europe by the Dutch ships in the 1600s; but now they are found everywhere in the world.

Their feathers are usually white, but there are other varieties of black, bluff, blue and grey.

Drakes weigh 3.2 kgs while the female ducks weigh 2.7 kgs. And live for 8 to 12 years.

They are a dual-purpose breed. They will give you delicious meat and will lay 100 to 130 eggs per year.

They are also used for ornamental purposes, due to their uniqueness and beauty.

Crested ducks are usually nervous ducks but the older they grow, they become calmer and friendly with people. They can make really good pets.

They thrive near water bodies because they are dabbling ducks. They sieve through mud, silt or gravel to find macroinvertebrates, zooplankton, clams and kelps. Therefore, they are recommended for people who live near water bodies, or someone who can make a small pond for them.

Cayuga

Cayuga duck originated from the USA in the 19th century. They are domestic ducks that are good for both egg and meat production and are sometimes used for ornamental purposes due to their unique black plumage.

They love to stay close to their home, which makes them easy to monitor and also good pets.

Cayuga duck are known for their black bill and their very dark feathers that give a greenish sheen when observed under light.

Cayugas are quiet ducks with a docile temperament. Friendly to people when hand raised. And they require extra protection because they are easily killed by predators such as cats, dogs, raccoons, etc.

Cayugas will give you a slice of delicious meat when slaughtered and lay 100 to 150 eggs per year. This breed is broody and will sit on their eggs for 28 days until they hatch. You can use them for brooding eggs for other ducks that don't brood. They weigh approximately 6 to 8 pounds and live up to 12 years when well taken care of.

This breed is also a lover of the pool. Have a fresh small water body around for them and keep it in a shaded area. Their very dark plumage absorbs a lot of heat that can make them so uncomfortable.

As they grow older, you will notice some white patches of feathers on them; don't be worried because this is absolutely normal. But one thing you should know is that during exhibitions, the ones with a lot of white feathers are usually disqualified.

33

Now that you have some knowledge on the duck breeds available to choose from, you may be very excited to go out and buy some duckling. If this is your first time raising ducklings, you may also be confused about how to go about choosing ducklings.

Let us look at that and a few other things.

Ducklings 101: The Ins And Outs of Duckling Selection & Care

How To Choose Ducklings

The best way to choose your ducklings is by choosing them from a place where you can observe them before buying them. This way, you can differentiate between healthy and unhealthy duckling. Look for a place where you will have time to observe duckling in their hatcheries before you purchase. To discover places where you can buy ducklings, just do a Google local search for duck hatcheries.

Examine the ducklings before you buy them. Look at how they behave, how they walk, and their activeness. Also, observe their body structures like their legs, wings, webbed feet, their back, and head, if they move about easily and swiftly etc. Proper examination will help you obtain a healthy and productive flock for yourself. If all the signs are good, then that's your signal to buy that duck.

Your choice of ducklings will also depend upon what you are looking to achieve with them. Some people raise ducks for pest control and exhibition, others for eggs and meat, while other people do it for commercial purposes. Depending on the discussion above on the different kinds of breeds, you will be able to make a good choice here.

How Many Ducklings Should You Raise As A Novice?

Are you worried about the number of ducks you are going to raise?

If your intention is to raise ducks that will live on their own, i.e. ducks that they will fend for themselves with minimal help from you, I would advise you to go for a maximum of 24 ducks.

Moreover, until you know everything about duck raising, which comes from personal experience, it would be better for you to start with a small flock. Begin with a flock of around six ducklings/ducks comprising of 1 drake or male duck and 5 female ducks. With this flock of 6 ducks, you will be able to get approximately 5-10 eggs per week. Drakes are very sexually active; they can overwhelm your female ducks sexually (sometimes to death); that's why it is recommended to have more female ducks than drakes. Ducks are very social group of birds, so that's why you must have a flock of them, because loneliness could kill them.

In addition, with the drake around, you will be getting fertile eggs, meaning you can still raise ducklings by your own instead of buying some. Starting with a small flock can help you determine whether you will go for more eggs or more meat. Eventually, you can use some of the eggs to raise ducklings in order to increase your flock.

How To Know A Male And Female Duck

It is usually hard to differentiate a male duckling from a female one. But there are simple ways to know the exact gender of your ducklings. They include:

✓ Look for a curled feather near the tail. The curled feather at the tail of a duck is also known as the sex feather. Drakes have a few feathers that are curled upwardly near the end of their tail; whereas the female ducks do not possess any curling at their tail, instead they have straightly pointed feathers (they lack the sex feather). This curled feather becomes noticeable when male ducks are aged between 8 to 16 weeks and stay on for life.

✓ You can also listen to the quacking of your ducks. You can do this by holding the tail of your duck gently until it quacks. A male duck will produce a soft but slightly rough quack while the female duck will produce a louder and harder quack. Female ducks are known to be noisier when compared to the male duck. The sound of the quack is pretty much more effective because it can be used to differentiate a male from a female duck when they are just a month old.

✓ Other ways that can be used to differentiate a male from a female duck include: observing the duck's plumage during mating. When mating, the male ducks seem to develop a brighter coloration in their plumage. This is done so as to attract female ducks. But when the mating season is over, the male duck will molt and lose his bright-colored plumage, looking more like their female counterparts.

Another method that can be used is observing the size of the ducks. Male ducks are usually larger in size when compared to their female counterparts of similar age. Male ducks have larger body structures like the head, the neck, their shanks and their overall body size. They even weigh heavier than the female ones.

When you study your ducks as you raise them, you will also notice that the bill color of the ducks of the same breed are different and also, the bill shape.

As you study your ducks more, you will notice more differences in the male and the female ducks.

How To Handle Your Ducklings After Buying Them

When handling your ducklings, the most important thing you should know is that the legs and wings are very fragile. If you mishandle them, you can easily hurt or even break their legs and wings. Avoid grabbing your duckling by their legs and wings. Instead, hold it firmly and gently at the base of the neck. Alternatively, you can hold it by holding its wings against its side with one hand holding each side of its body while a thumb is over each wing.

If you are moving your duck through a longer distance, make sure you tie their legs together, find a basket or a crate (a breathable one), put them inside, and close the cover. Thereafter, feel free to move your duck around.

After you have brought your ducks home, ensure that you regularly carry them or handle them, to get them used to you or other people. This will make it easier to handle them in the future when you will be examining them for diseases, taking them to their houses or when you want to butcher some for meals. Regular contact with your ducks will build their personality towards being friendly to people, hence, making good pets.

Have you bought your ducklings yet? Before you go out and spend some money on some ducklings, you need to know that your ducks need a place to stay when you bring them home. Let us look at everything duck housing.

It is important to note and remember that while choosing duck breeds, you should go for ducklings that fit your end goal and factor in things like your space and resources.

Duck Housing 101: Choosing A Place To Raise Your Duck/Lings

"Be like a duck. Calm on the surface, but always paddling like the dickens underneath"

- Michael Caine

When you're thinking about where to raise ducklings, you probably have several ideas of where to locate their housing. If you have an idea, that is great. However, you should note that the best place to house your ducklings or ducks is as close to your house as is possible.

If you're the DIY (do-it-yourself) kind of person and feel you can be good at making your own duck house, let us look at what you need to consider when building a home for your ducks.

Considerations When Building Duck's Shelter

Location

Basically, your duck's shelter should be at a place that provides shade for your ducks on hot days or during summer. It should be a place where they can hide during windy,

41

snowy, and rainy seasons. If possible, place their housing near where there is enough of the kinds of food ducks like to feed on, i.e. a place that is close to a source of water or even a pod so they can easily swim.

Locate your duck's shelter at a gently sloping land as well. Flat areas won't have adequate draining capability, whereas steep areas will make it harder to build a nest for your ducks.

Your duck's shelter should also be closer to you as possible. This will enable you to monitor them easily. When a predator or any harm comes towards your duck, you can easily jump into action and save them. But if you happen to be far, even a hawk or a raccoon can come around, hunt and pick your baby duckling without you even noticing.

Also, it is important to locate your duck's shelter at a place near your compost pile. As we have learned earlier, ducks cannot control their bowel movements because they lack the lower sphincter at the end of their gut. This makes them to poop all the time, continuously. Having a shelter close to the compost pile will make it easier for you to transport their droppings easily over a short distance, and preserve it for a while as manure.

To top it all, make sure you choose a quiet and calm area to build a pen for your duck, both for staying indoors and playing outside.

Predator Proof

Duck housing can be as simple or as elaborate as you may choose. Whether you change a small doghouse into a duck house or build a custom shed, the most important thing you should consider **is whether the house is predictor proof**. Many predators find duck meat and eggs so yummy. Some of them are our own domesticated animals like cats and dogs; others are wild animals like foxes raccoons, coyotes, weasels, and also snakes. And to make matters riskier for us, ducks are quiet, heavy flightless birds; therefore, it is very easy for predators to get to them.

When building your duck's coop, ensure that you build it in a manner that can protect your ducks from any sorts of danger, particularly at night when you are not available to watch over them.

To ensure protection, build a fence around your coop, ensure that the fence is small enough to bar any predator, even the snakes. Since ducks sleep on the floor, ensure the floor is made of a hard foundation like cement, bricks or wood, to prevent predators from digging through. Cover the windows and the ventilation vents with a wire mesh as well.

Pick up eggs immediately they are laid. Ducks are careless layers; they lay their eggs about anywhere. Monitor them closely and pick up their eggs regularly before they attract predators.

To ensure all your ducks are safe, watch them during the evening while they are entering their coop and ensure that their numbers and health are in order.

Below is an example of a predator-proof pen with fences all around:

Train Your Ducks To Return To Their Pen

Training your duck to return to their pen is very important. This is because it will protect them from predators and will also help you to avoid losing your ducks. Some ducks will spend the night outside or by the pond and will not easily get or know the purpose of the pen you have built for them.

So to make them aware of the purpose and the time to get to their coop, you must train them.

You can do this just by the way you train a dog. Associate a sound to feeding. Make a unique sound while feeding your ducks and ensure that you feed them only inside their pen. Do this every evening at around the same time, and after some time they will be so used to their coop, to a point where they won't be able to sleep anywhere else but inside their coop.

Shelter Size

Before you start thinking of how fancy you want your duck house to be, figure out how spacious it needs to be. It is always advisable to give each duck a floor space of four square feet. This is because ducks sleeps on piles of bedding on the floor. This requires some space for them to be comfortable. Also, allow for at least 10 square feet or more for each duck on the outside. Ducks love to spend their time outside, to forage and also to run around as exercise. Adequate run space is very necessary.

The shelter should also be large enough to let you walk in and clean with ease. Adequate space will also enable you to store some little food for the next day or week for your ducks in little shelves you may build inside.

Breeds like Muscovy ducks that like to perch will also require a taller shelter as compared to other ducks.

Shelter size should also be larger enough to allow room for more ducks because eventually, your ducks will give rise to more ducklings.

Flooring

A duck house can be built on the ground. However, to avoid predators digging to access them, it is advisable to build on a wooden or cement floor. In addition, you can cover the floor with an inexpensive vinyl for easy cleaning and for keeping the floor dry, especially after you leave water overnight.

Furthermore, ensure that whatever you use for your flooring is waterproof - to withstand their watery droppings. This will make it easy for you to clean and keep it dry. Gravel or clay can get muddy, hence, making the ducks' pen really uncomfortable and prone to microorganisms and diseases.

The flooring should also be smooth. This is because a smooth floor will prevent scarring of the ducks' webbed feet while they walk around the house.

Bedding

Ducks prefer straws as their bedding material. This is mainly because straw has wonderful insulating properties, especially during colder seasons. Apart from straw, you can use pine shavings, hay or a raised wire mesh above the floor.

Of all the bedding materials you have heard of or been advised to use, the best of the best are, as stated earlier, straws and shavings. Straws last longer, do not get wet easily, and are easy on the webbed feet of ducks. Straws also have the ability to maintain their shape for a very long time. Ducks can use these straws to build a nest or nesting areas to lay eggs, and it will remain so, without changing. In addition, straws are known to produce little dust and compost easily when taken to the compost pile as manure.

Shavings are also recommended because they are able to absorb moisture as much as they are comfortable on the ducks' feet.

Ensure always to recycle your duck's pen bedding as often as possible. There poop tends to contain a lot of moisture, and within a short while, the shavings will start to get wet, a little mud-like, and very uncomfortable for your ducks feet. Wet shavings are also known to attract microorganisms. Keeping your bedding dry, warm, and fresh as always will improve the health, the wellbeing and the comfort of your ducks in their pen.

Ventilation-

Build a house that is 3 ft. high with vents to allow a good flow of air. Naturally, ducks emit a lot of moisture when breathing, or through their dropping (ducks droppings contain a lot of moisture because they pee through their poop). So if that moisture does not escape, it can bring molds and mildewed on the duck bedding causing aspergillosis or frostbitten feet during winter.

Include extra windows with hinged shutters that can be closed or opened as needed and according to the weather. Cover all vents and windows with ½-inch hardware cloth to prevent predators from accessing the ducks. Locate the window at least a foot from the ground to prevent predictors from seeing ducks from outside.

The ventilation you have designed for your ducks' pen should also be able to protect them from the prevailing wind. Know the common direction of the flow of wind in your area and design your pen and the ventilation vents accordingly.

A well-ventilated pen will also help you from overusing your available chicken bedding. This is because a well-ventilated pen will keep the pen dry all the time, minimizing the dampening of the bedding.

Even though ducks are good regulators of their body temperature, by storing warm air under their feathers, the building of your ventilation will also depend on the season. During hot seasons, ensure your vents are high enough to enable ease of flow of air within the pen hence reducing humidity inside the ducks' house. In cold seasons, the vent should be lower enough to regulate the temperature inside the ducks' pen.

You should also know that ventilation goes hand in hand with temperature regulation. You can control the temperature in your ducks' shelter by managing ventilation. Temperature control is more critical when the ducks are still very young. But when they grow older, they will be able to control their own body temperature through any weather.

Entrance/Exit-

Ducks love to do things in groups. They walk together, eat together and play together. They are very social, as you will observe when you start raising them. To ensure harmony, peace, and good relations among your ducks, make sure the pop door to your ducks' house should be wide to allow two ducks to enter or exit at once. Ducks have a habit of pushing and shoving. If the door is too small, they can be stuck. On the door, use a predator-proof latch; bear in mind that raccoons can glide a deadbolt and lift the latches. Therefore, using something like an eye hook is advisable. Ducks are heavy, close to the ground, flightless, and relatively weak and short legs; therefore, if the house is not on the ground (which is highly recommended), ducks will need a ramp to use to get in and out of the house. The ramp should be wide and ridged. A smooth ramp can be slippery to your ducks when they come out of their pool. If you choose a narrow ramp, add railings to help them keep their balance. The ramp should not be steep. It should be slightly inclined to enable the ducks to walk through with ease.

Nesting Boxes

Most ducks make their own nests from their bedding material, mostly straw, at a dark corner of their pen. But it is encouraged to make your duck get used to a nesting box. A nesting box is important because it will enable you to collect a clean, fresh egg, without any cracks: the eggs will be much safer from predators, and free from the intense heat from the sun.

Put the nesting box on the floor, because ducks don't fly. Add some straws on the nesting box and place it in a dark warm corner for your duck. Always ensure that the nests are clean, dry, comfortable for your duck and large enough for the mother duck, the eggs, and the ducklings when they will be hatching.

The appropriate size of a nesting box should be 30 cm by 30 cm and by 40 cm in height. Then the bedding material that you use (straw or pine shavings) should be placed inside the nesting box to a depth of around 7 cm.

When refreshing the bedding of your ducks' pen, do the same to the bedding also in the nesting box. Always ensure it is dry, clean and comfortable for your bird.

Water

You cannot raise a duck without enough water.

Ducks love water.

They need water for mating, breeding, drinking, entertainment, keeping off external parasites. Also, some breeds are dabbling ducks, that is, they obtain their feed from water. They do this by sieving through the mud or silt, and eating kelps or even planktons from water.

If you have a pond or live close to a water body like a lake or river, you are lucky. But if you don't have a pond or you don't live near a water body, you are lucky as well because building a little swimming pool for your ducks is easy. You might as well buy a kiddie pool, or use an old bathtub as their swimming ground.

You can also build a 2-meter wide concrete pool, which is 0.3 meters deep, is enough for your ducks. Ensure that you have good drainage or you might as well fetch this water when it is dirty, and use it to water your garden plants. Ducks swimming water can be very nutritious to your plants because they also poop in there while they swim.

Apart from swimming, ducks need a lot of drinking water. Whenever they eat, they will require some water to wash down their food, failure to which they might choke and even die. Ensure then their drinking water is outside their sleeping shelter to prevent dampening of their bedding material, high humidity, and higher temperatures for the little ducklings.

Keep their water clean at all times to prevent blockage of their nasal passages. Also, keep every waterer 3 cm from one another to allow for drinking space between large adult ducks.

Feeders

There are no feeders made exactly for ducks right now, but you can use the ones made for chicken. Ducks need more feeding space than chickens. Allow 12 cm space between feeders of each duck.

It is advised that the feeders are placed significantly closer to the waterers. Because after feeding, ducks will always need water to drink.

shutterstock.com • 1420607483

Lighting

Finally, one last factor you need to consider when building your ducks' pen is lighting.

Lighting is very essential because it will increase the length of the laying period of your ducks. It is important to supplement the days light with artificial light for 14 to 17 hours of overall lighting period during the day's 24 hour period. Failure to supplement light, egg production will depend upon the diurnal lighting period, which can be shorter sometimes, hence, low production.

Adding artificial light will enable your duck to lay eggs continuously for 7 to 12 months a year.

So how will you maintain a 14 hour lighting period?

Turn on the lights a few hours before dawn and turn off the light a few hours after dusk. You can use automated programs to do this for you, or you can do it by yourself every morning, as it will also help you be an early riser. Ensure that you maintain a constant turning on and off of your artificial light. And since ducks lay most of their eggs in the morning hours and in the evening, you will be able to easily collect these eggs from their nest every day.

Good lighting is also known to stimulate sexual activeness between the drakes and the ducks.

Even though ducks are known to be nocturnal, light will be essential for ducklings to feed and drink during the night, before they develop like the adult ducks.

Below is an example of a simple duck house with a swimming trough.

Basic Duck Care

Like most ducklings or any other growing creature, ducklings need warmth and a safe environment when they are small. To that end, use a heat lamp with a bulb of 40-100 watts. You can change the bulb in accordance with the ducks' behavior. For example, when they are huddling under the lamp, you should increase the wattage of the bulb, if they are scattered and looks like they're panting, you should lower the wattage.

An ideal brooder for raising ducklings for the first few days should be a box or crate. When they become big and outgrow the box, you can think of building an outdoor coop similar to that of chicken coops, as we have just looked at.

Ducks need an environment that meets their behavioral, physical, and social needs. Ducks are social pets; they should be raised in such a way that their needs are completely taken care of.

Ducks are also curious birds, you need to allow them space to roam freely, forage, and find water bodies of their choice, but closer ones. They love to forage in the garden in such for bugs, slugs, worms, weeds etc. You will find small holes dug by their bills, in such for worms. If you have a vegetable garden, like for kales, spinach etc., don't allow your ducks in that garden. This is because they will eat up all your vegetables before you even realize it.

However, you can raise your ducks in various conditions ranging from a backyard coop, which is suitable for a few ducks to a bigger shelter suitable for large flocks meant for business/commercial duck farming. Regardless, there are crucial basic requirements that should be met to keep their health in check.

Let Us Examine Some Of These Duck Standards/Requirements.

Duck care standards- The environment in which ducks are raised should be designed in such a way that it promotes the overall well being of the ducks and protects the ducks from any distress and discomfort.

Basic duck care requirements include:

- When your ducks are young, before they reach five weeks of age, do not allow these ducks out into the water. Let them grow first, develop feathers, and become stable and strong enough, then, let them into a pool. This is at about 6 weeks of age. Ducklings also are unable to produce waterproofing oil on their skins until they are about 4 weeks of age. Exposing them to water bodies at a very young age can be dangerous to them. This is because the water can make their skin soft and vulnerable to scratches, they can get so cold, or they might even drown because they are not yet experienced swimmers. When they get chilled, they can get weak and therefore drown. Make sure you supervise them all the time when introducing them to swimming.

- It is also very important to keep your young ducklings' warm and dry at all times. Place them inside a small cage and provide a heating mechanism of about 25 to 30° C. The best way to achieve this is through a light bulb during the day and a little safe temperature moderating heater at night. Ensure to keep them warm until they are six weeks of age. After this time, they will be able to control their own body temperature.

- Also, when your ducks are still young (little ducklings), ensure that the floor at which they stay in or walk on is not slippery at all. A slippery floor will make your little ducklings develop a serious condition known as splay legs or spraddle legs. Splay leg is a deformity in which the ducks' legs will point to the sides instead of pointing forward. This deformity can last a lifetime if not corrected. It will make waking or swimming difficult and sometimes, it can make it impossible. So for a healthy flock, make the ground rough, use beddings or anything that can provide a grip to your little ducklings' developing feet.

- You must be able to know the simple ways of protecting your ducks against extreme weather conditions. Hot seasons such as the very high summer temperatures or the extreme cold seasons such as winter must be withstood easily by your ducks through your help.

You should also protect your ducks from predators as well, just by the ways we have discussed above.

- Your ducks will also require a clean, dry sheltered spot in your compound (it can be the ducks' run or under a tree), that they can use as a retreat when they need rest from swimming all day, foraging, or just for relaxing. This clean, dry spot will help your birds to keep their bodies warm and their skin intact; thereby, helping them to avoid injuries that might occur.

- Inside the ducks' pen, ensure that you provide adequate lighting at an appropriate wattage.

- Give them meals that provide all their nutritional requirements every day. A healthy meal will help ducklings grow and mature, adult ducks to be more productive and improve the overall immunity of your ducks.

Also, provide clean water for drinking at all times. It is recommended to keep their waterers a short distance from their feeders because, like I have said before, ducks can, at times, be very messy. They will splash water on their feeds if they are put closer together. A distant waterer will also give them a chance to walk a little as form of exercise and leave space for other ducks to feed too.

- Buy small quantities of duck food regularly unless you have a large flock. Buying a lot of food at once is not advisable because while storing them, these feeds will slowly lose their vitamins with time. Also, avoid exposing the meals to the sun or heat as they will also rapidly break down the vitamins in the feed.

Keep the feeds in a cool, dry, and airtight place to avoid the formation of molds. Metallic containers are also known to encourage molds growth in the feeds.

Check the expiry dates of the feeds and avoid giving your ducks expired feeds.

- And finally, protect your ducks from diseases by observing other basic duck care requirements.

Ducks are naturally strong birds; bird diseases known to affect chickens and turkey do not easily affect them.

Like other domestic animals, ducks need to eat too. In the next chapter, we shall look at and get familiar with everything duck feeding.

How big you build you duck house will depend on why you want to raise ducks. If you want a few ducks, you don't need a large pool of water to keep your ducklings happy. On the other hand, if you have many ducks, you may require a large pool.

The Ins And Outs Of Duck Feeding

"It doesn't matter if you're born in a duck yard, so long as you are hatched from a swan's egg!"

- Hans Christian Andersen, the Ugly Duckling

Although ducks eat many things and forage for themselves when they get bigger, one of their favorite type of food is pellets. You should make a point of feeding your duckling pellets, especially when they are young.

Here is a note for you: UNDER NO CIRCUMSTANCE SHOULD YOU FEED YOUR DUCK OR DUCKLINGS JUNK FOOD. Unfortunately, many people feed their duck with bread, breadcrumbs, and junk food. This often causes algae and various other ailments.

Ducklings often make a mess when they're eating. Therefore, you should take a lot of care when feeding them. Moreover, a ducklings' droppings are wet and prolific. Therefore, because they may poop in their food, you should make a point of replacing their feed on a daily basis.

Further, you should construct their feeders and water containers in such a way that it allows for easy access at all times. That being the case, let us outline some of the core feeding guidelines you should follow in terms of feeding to ensure that they grow strong.

Feeding

Duckling should have easy access to their food on a 24-hour basis for the critical first two weeks. They should be fed a starter feed with approximately 18-20% protein. The feed can be in mash form or even crumble form.

If you settle on mash feed, wet the mash to make it easier for them to eat. If you prefer to feed them mash, replace it several times a day to prevent spoilage. A few examples of feed you can feed your ducklings include broiler starter, chick starter, turkey starter or duck/waterfowl starter. Take a lot of care when feeding them with higher protein level feed as it can result in physical damages such as angel wings, overweight birds and other growth defects.

Angel wings is a condition whereby the wings of your ducks become crooked as they grow. This happens because too much protein will lead to rapid development of ducks' bones to a point where others overgrow, especially in the wing area, hence becoming crooked.

So how do you feed them proteins? For the first two weeks of their life, feed your ducklings 18 to 20 percent of proteins then switch to 16 percent of proteins for the next 6 to 8 weeks.

You should never feed ducklings with any layer feed since it has high calcium level, which can result to damages or death.

Another important factor to take into account when feeding your ducklings is this: do not feed them any meal that is medicated. Most meal producers add medication in their meals, like a medication for coccidiosis etc. Ducklings eat a lot. Therefore, when you give them a medicated meal, they will overdose on that drug, leading to serious health issues or at times death.

So I will advise you to watch the ingredients on your ducks' feed carefully and take home, that which is free of medications. One thing we have learned is that ducks are hardy birds, hence they are resistant to most of these diseases.

Ducklings also need niacin in their meals while growing. Niacin helps in strengthening ducks bones as they develop. Ducks grow pretty fast; hence, they will require a lot more niacin as compared to chickens. You can add niacin to their meals by adding **brewer's yeast** to their pellets.

It is also important to introduce your ducklings to green vegetables, grass or other herbs to enrichen their diet at an early age. Making them used to greens and herbs will make it easier for them to become foragers when they grow up. Put some of these herbs in a water trough and let them eat from there because while they swim and enjoy themselves, they will learn how to fetch herbs from water bodies. Hence, they will become excellent dabbling ducks.

Make the feeds of your ducklings slightly wet, to give them an ease while swallowing.

For adults ducks (21 weeks and older), feed them with finisher and layers feed. Ducks are good foragers; they can still feed themselves in the yard, drain or supplementary green feed/ grass.

For laying ducks, you should look for layers or a breeder diet that is 16 to 17 percent protein. Also, make sure they have enough calcium for good healthy and strong eggs. Calcium can be obtained from shelled grit.

For drakes and other non-laying ducks, 14 percent protein meal is enough for them. Reduce the amount of calcium as well.

Mix the ducks feed (which is usually 20 percent protein) with oats to reduce the percentage of the protein. You can do this by adding 20 grams of oat grains to 80 grams of your ducks feed to make a 16 percent protein feed.

Adult ducks do not require niacin. Therefore, after they reach 20 weeks of age, stop adding brewer's yeast to their food.

Occasionally, during their day, you can add some treats to your ducks. These treats include: chopped lettuce, salad mixes, vegetable trimming or peels, nuts, rice, corns or peace, grapes, wheat, barley or other grains, uncooked oats, milo seeds, nuts without salt or coatings, earthworms, mealworms etc.

Tips For Feeding Ducks

- Do not continue to feed your ducks when they appear uninterested. They won't eat the excess food, leaving behind uneaten food which can attract unwanted pests.

- Do not overfeed your ducks.

- Provide them food that are small sized. Ducks swallow food; they don't have teeth to chew with. Large pieces can choke they as they eat

- Be wary of wary of other large waterfowl such as swans and geese, as they can become aggressive to your ducks as you feed them.

- Provide food for your ducks at a clean surface. A place with litter, can contain tiny nails, sharp rocks or thorns, to say the least, that can hurt your ducks as the eat.

- In relation to creating a feeding schedule for your ducks and ducklings, the recommended feeding schedules are as follows.

What Not To Feed Your Ducks

- Do not feed your ducks any medicated meals.

- Drakes or other non-laying duck should not be fed oyster shells, as these may lead to kidney problems like kidney failure.

- Do not feed your ducks expired feeds, moldy feeds or rotten ones.

- Do not give your ducks bread crumbs, fast foods like chips, popcorn, donuts, crackers and sweets.

Age	0-2 Weeks	2-8 Weeks	8-20 Weeks	First Egg
Protein level	18-20%	16-18%	15-16%	16-18%

After 8 weeks, you can feed them twice a day, i.e. morning and evening. At this stage, they consume an average of 12.5 grams of feed up to 20 weeks of age. From there, the consumption differs from 120 grams and above per day.

If you intend to raise ducks specifically for meat, the feed eaten will depend on factors like quality of food, method of management and strain of duck. You can use the table below to access their average feed consumption rate.

Age (Weeks)	Feed Per Week (Kgs)	Cumulative (Kg)
0-1	0.15	0.15
1	0.40	0.55
2	0.75	1.30
3	0.95	2.25

4	1.00	3.25
5	1.30	4.55
6	1.65	6.20
7	1.80	8.00
8	1.60	9.60

Feed conversion ratios: The feed ratios for ducks breed for meat purposes is around 2.5:1 until their ducklings are marketable at 6 weeks of age weighing around 3kgs.

Grit

Grit are very small stones, sand or even dirt. As we have learned earlier, ducks do not have teeth. So how do they grind up what they eat? When ducks swallow food, these food will move down their gut to a part known as the gizzard (sometimes also referred to as the second stomach). In the gizzard, the small stones or sand swallowed by ducks will be used to grind up the food particles into very tiny particles that can be easily digested.

So you must ensure that your ducks have access to grit at all times, even inside their pen. Because it is very essential for their well-being.

For the laying ducks, you can purchase grit with crushed oyster shells. They will provide calcium that will make the egg shells strong and healthy.

Water

Allow me to ask you a question. Why do you think ducks require a pond? I'm almost certain that a majority of people just pronounced swimming purposes as the correct answer. This answer is Ok and correct. However, that's not all ducks require water for. Let me amaze you; a week old duck can drink even half a gallon of water in 5days' time, at 7 weeks, he or she can drink half a gallon of water in a day.

Make sure your ducks have plenty of fresh water for their healthy growth. For ducklings, use a shallow dish and add some pebbles to prevent them from submerging and drowning.

If you provide insufficient water to your ducks, they will end up choking every time they eat. As indicated earlier, ducks should dip their heads in water to keep their mucus membrane moist; this is because as they eat, their beaks grab foods or mud, therefore, they need water to swish around in their beaks to clear it off food and dirt.

You should note that if ducks don't dip their head in water, they may suffer blindness. This is because their eyes get scaly and crusty hence they often wash them in their water container or pond.

Use plastics or stainless steel as water containers both for drinking and for swimming. Metallic containers can leach heavy metals into the water causing toxicity in water. When ducks drink such water, both your health and their health are at risk.

Wash drinking containers daily. Since ducks are known to be messy, they will poop in their drinking containers making it difficult for other ducks to drink the same water. Dirty waterers can also encourage buildup of bacteria, parasites and other microorganisms, also algae. These material can cause serious health issues to your ducks.

Swimming facilities are not necessary, but if you find it necessary, you can provide them with a pool outside. To limit wastage of eggs, release them to the pool after 10.am when they have laid most eggs.

How you choose to raise your ducks or ducklings, .e. how you feed them, where you house them etc. will determine how healthy your ducks turn out to

be. Take great care in providing your ducks with the proper care they need to flourish into strong healthy ducks. Luckily, this chapter has equipped you with everything you need to feed and care for your ducks. With this knowledge, nothing stands on your way to raising strong and healthy ducks.

Duck Health 101: Everything You Need To Do To Raise Strong And Healthy Ducks

"We will not duck the tough issues, we will lead"

- Paul Ryan

Keeping your ducks healthy requires you to take the necessary steps required to prevent disease outbreaks. It requires that in cases where your ducks are infected, you should administer appropriate treatment immediately to avoid morbidity and mortality.

Fortunately, it is easy to notice signs of an infected duck. This is because when your ducks are healthy and normal, they show signs of good health. Though it often depends on sex, age, and breed. Some of the crucial indications of a healthy duck are as follows: vigorous movements while distracted, good body posture, good plumage, clean and healthy skin, well-formed feet and hanks', preening, effective walking, clear bright eyes and active feeding and drinking.

On the other hand, sick ducks show early symptoms of ailments or stress as follows; huddling, head pulled into the body, lack of preening, changes in water and feed intake,

75

diarrhea, general inactivity, drooping of the eyelids, problems with sitting and walking, puffy head, lower in weight and squinted eyes.

That being the case, it is easier for you to distinguish between when your ducks are sick/stressed and when they are healthy.

Undoubtedly, your ducks will get sick. What you do when one duck gets sick determines if the other ducks, i.e. if you have many ducks, also get sick. This also determines how fatal some diseases can be on your brood.

What To Do When Your Ducks Catch Diseases?

There are several known diseases common in ducks. Infections such as:

Coccidiosis in young ducks. Most ducks are resistant to this disease and are rarely affected. And if they get it, the disease will go away on its own without treatment.

It is caused by coccidian protozoa, which is a parasite spread through the fecal-oral route. It is characterized by severe enteritis expressed through hemorrhagic diarrhea, mucoid discharge, weight loss, reduced appetite and depression.

This disease can be prevented through proper hygiene and ventilation, vaccine, disinfection of ducks' pen occasionally, etc.

Treatment is done using sulphonamides in ducks that take longer to recover on their own.

Botulism comes from eating things like dead rats or birds. The dead rats or ducks most times possess a bacteria known as *Clostridium botulinum*. This bacteria produces toxins that cause paralysis in the entire duck's body. Parts such as the wings, legs, neck, the eyelids, and more lose their function. It also comes with constant diarrhea.

There is no treatment for this disease, so most ducks will sadly die. But you can try to manage the condition, and the duck will recover by itself. Feed and water them, support them while swimming, and if it recoups, good for you.

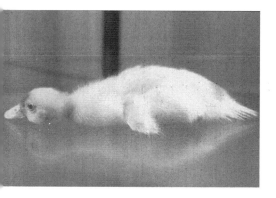

Duck viral enteritis (duck plague) is usually obtained from wild birds. It is spread through the fecal-oral route or when your healthy ducks come in contact with contaminated surfaces or water. It is highly contagious in a flock foraging or living together, and is usually characterized by sudden death. This is because the virus will cause vascular damage, internal hemorrhage, lymphoid gland lesions, liver necrosis, severe diarrhea, etc. When the internal homeostasis is interfered with in this manner, the duck will definitely die.

It is caused by a virus known as *Anatid alpha herpesvirus*. And it is capable of going through a latent period (asymptomatic period). Even when a duck recovers, it can still be a carrier, and an outbreak can arise any time. I would recommend that you quarantine infected ducks and perform culling. There is no treatment available yet.

Prevention is only through vaccination in prone areas.

Angel wings is a condition caused by excess protein intake, carbohydrates, and sugars with a deficiency in vitamins and minerals while the duck is young and still developing. The feathers grow faster than the wing structure. The heavy feathers will then make the wings of your duck will become twisted and pointing out sideways instead of lying flat.

Ducklings from 8 to 12 weeks are more at risk of this condition.

In young ducks, damage can be reversed through proper feeding and wrapping the wings to the body of the duck for some time.

This condition is irreversible in mature ducks.

It can be prevented by lowering the protein diet, lots of exercise by allowing your ducks outside often and adding greens to their diet.

The image below is an example of an angel wing;

Aspergillosis which is caused by fungi that can come from grains harvested while still wet or by inhalation of aspergillus fungi spores in contaminated material. The fungi invade the respiratory system, which include the trachea, lungs and the alveoli, making breathing difficult through suffocation. Ducklings and immunocompromised adult ducks are the ones at risk. There is no known treatment, but it can prevented through proper ventilation and good sanitary conditions. Below is an example of a duckling suffering from aspergillosis:

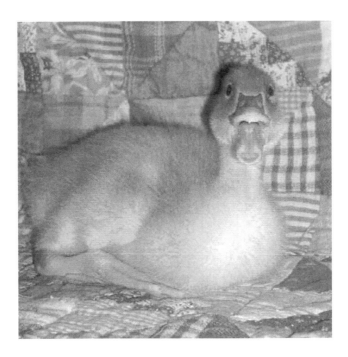

Bumble-foot which is a large or swollen discolored area in the ducks' feet with pus. It can be brought about through injuries or abrasion in the ducks' feet, lack of enough swimming, obesity, and extra foot pressure. Once a cut develops, a bacteria known as *Staphylococcus aureus* enters through the injured spot and causes this infection. Antibiotics such as a 22.7mg of Baytril pill per day will take away this infection. But if it gets serious, surgical removal might be the only choice available.

To prevent this disease from occurring, eliminate all rough surfaces and pointed nails, sticks or rocks, from the places your ducks usually forage. You can also prevent it by providing proper bedding material, separating the infected ducks from the healthy ones, disinfecting the coop, and if you have perching ducks like the Muscovy, lower the roosts to a few centimeters from the ground.

Below is how a bumblefoot looks like;

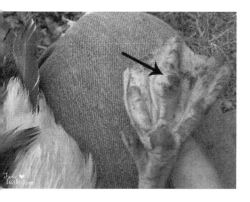

Egg bound disease can be caused low calcium, low vitamin D and low protein levels in the meals you provide for your ducks. Low calcium levels will make the eggshell too soft to be laid. Other causes can be due to an infection in the reproductive organ or a shapeless egg.

In egg bound disease, the egg gets trapped in the lower reproductive tract of the duck, leading to obstruction in oviposition (Your duck will no longer be able to lay more eggs).

When you start seeing symptoms such as a swollen abdomen, lethargy, abrupt stoppage in egg production, fluffed feathers, and constipation, you should immediately take your duck to the vet. You can also cure your duck on your own by lubricating the cloaca with a KY jelly (a water-based lubricant) gently, then place the duck in a warm pool of water for an hour. If doesn't come out within an hour, try massaging the egg out gently while adding more lubrication.

Failure to treat the duck within 48 hours can lead to death.

You can prevent this disease through proper balanced diet with calcium and vitamin D supplementation.

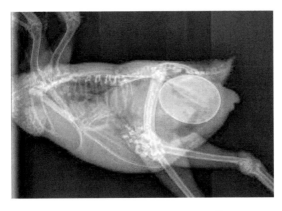

When ducks get sick, most duck owners always rush to administer antibiotics. Although this is sound advice, you should never do so without the assistance of a qualified vet. This is because duck are very similar to chicks or chicken. As such, their diseases spread in the same way: through contact. What may start as a simple cold in one duck could end up costing you your whole brood.

Fortunately, as earlier, with a simple internet search, you can find many vets in your local area.

As we know, prevention is always better than cure. Although your ducks will undoubtedly get sick, there are things you can do to ensure that your ducks avoid getting sick.

Let us look at a few of these things.

Disease Prevention

Disease prevention for ducks follows the same blueprint as that of any other domesticated foul. In fact, duck disease prevention does not differ from that of any other domestic bird. Being a duck owner, you must be diligent in these three main areas to keep your duck safe from any diseases.

Try to establish and maintain a bio-security program in charge of preventing the introduction of any ailments within the premises of your ducks. This includes prohibiting any admission of possible sources of contagious agents. This could manifest in the form of other animals, fowls or sick ducks. In cases where it is necessary to bring live ducks in your farm, make sure they are from diseases-free sources. You should also take time to observe them before they join your large duck congregation.

- Additionally, you should restrict the entry of trucks, people and poultry materials that can carry any disease. This could be in the form of boots or other farm equipment. Take disinfection measures before entering the premises of your ducks.

- Vaccinate your ducks against known contagious diseases. In case there is an outbreak of a common duck disease, you can protect yours by administering appropriate vaccines at the right time.

- Minimize environmental stresses for your ducks by doing the following; provide good management, providing proper housing that has good ventilation, and nutrition.

- Ensure high sanitation standards. Always clean the duck pen, their waterers and feeders, refresh their swimming pool and also change their bedding when they start to get wet and filled with droppings.

- Separate the healthy flocks from the ones that appear sick. By doing this, you will prevent the spread of diseases from one duck to the other.

- Keep the duck house spacious enough for free and easy air circulation around the pen. Foul air is swept out and replaced with fresh comfortable air.

- Disinfect the ducks' pen once a month if you can. This will help you to kill any developing microorganism inside the pen.

- Control rodents. Make sure rats or mice do not live anywhere close to the ducks' pen. Rodents can carry some infectious diseases that can be fatal to your ducks.

- Lastly, and more importantly, provide your ducks with a balanced healthy diet. You will be able to prevent 70 percent of diseases through proper diet.

As we have seen thus far, your decision to go with duck raising was well-founded. I am hopeful that thus far, you have gained some knowledge on how raise strong, healthy ducks.

You should note that working with any type of animal is not easy. However, with the knowledge we have learned thus far, you can become an expert duck farmer/owner. As we stated earlier, ducks are susceptible to various diseases, infections, and parasites. As we have seen, the best way to ensure that your ducks grow strong and healthy is by providing them with the proper shelter, water and food. Further, you should ensure that their living space is clean and dry.

Again, it is undoubtedly that your ducklings may still fall ill regardless of how cautious or careful you are. Such diseases include: Curled Toes, Duck Virus Hepatitis, Duck Virus Enteritis, Coccidiosis, Slipped Wing, Aspergillosis, Wet Feather, Avian Cholera, Botulism and Worms

In this regard, this resource has great information on the top ten diseases you should look out for as you raise your ducks.

https://www.offthegridnews.com/how-to-2/10-common-illness-foundin-ducklings/

At this point, everything you have learned thus far has equipped you with all the knowledge you need and require to raise strong, healthy ducks. At this point, the only thing left is you implementing everything we have learned. In the next chapter, I

shall show you how to implement everything we have learned.

How To Put This Information Into Action

"We are all born ignorant, but one must work hard to remain stupid"

- Benjamin Franklin

At this point in our book/learning process, you have learned everything there is to learn about ducklings. Subsequently, you have also learned everything there is to learn about raising healthy ducks. We have learned everything from different duck breeds, how to care for them and where to house them. We have also looked at how to feed your ducks, keep them happy, and protect them from diseases.

As stated earlier, the only thing left is for you to implement whatever we have learned. In this respect, here is how to apply what you have learned thus far.

Before going out to buy ducklings, determine your 'why' Your why in this case is the reason driving you towards duck raising. Once you determine this, move to determine how much space and resources you have at your disposal. Going through this step will help you answer questions such as where to build your duck house, how to provide them with their entertainment water, and how to protect them from the various factors affecting their lives.

When it comes to building a home for your ducks, your 'why' will determine how big your duck house is. If you want to raise duck for commercial purposes, you require a lot of space and a big water source. However, for duck pets, a small space and a kiddie pool is adequate.

When it comes to feeding, although ducks are natural foragers, how you choose to feed your ducks determines how healthy they turn out. Feeding your ducks the appropriate amount of food they need to flourish is an important step towards raising healthy ducks. And remember that it is very important not to feed your ducks bread or sandwiches as people usually do.

When your ducks get sick, even if it's a single duck, don't be quick to reach for antibiotics. Instead, have your local vet on speed dial. The reason for this is that without proper care and precaution, a common ailment like one of those on the list of 10 common duck ailments could prove fatal to your entire brood.

Conclusion

I hope this book was able to help you to understand how to raise healthy ducks easily with confidence.

The next step is to implement what you've learned in this book to raise healthy ducks.

Printed in Great Britain
by Amazon

14867303R00052